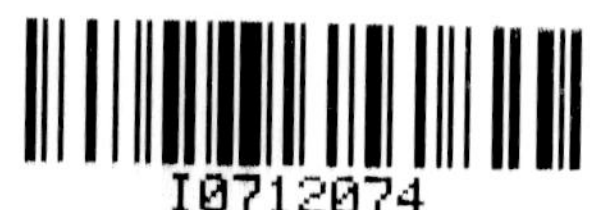

For the most curious child I know! I dedicate this little book full of mysteries and fantasies to you! Have a good time!

Beatriz Silva

2024

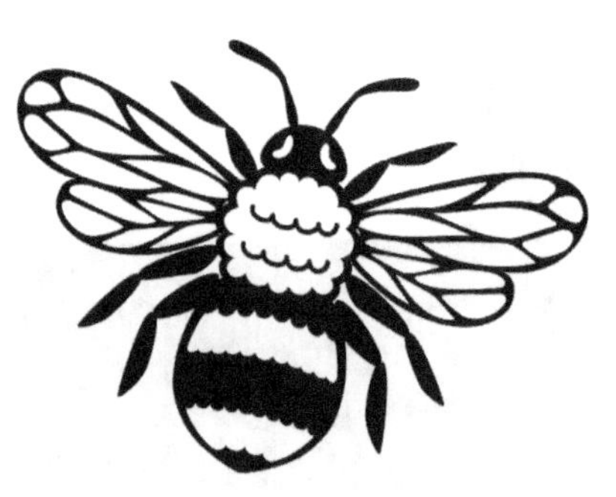
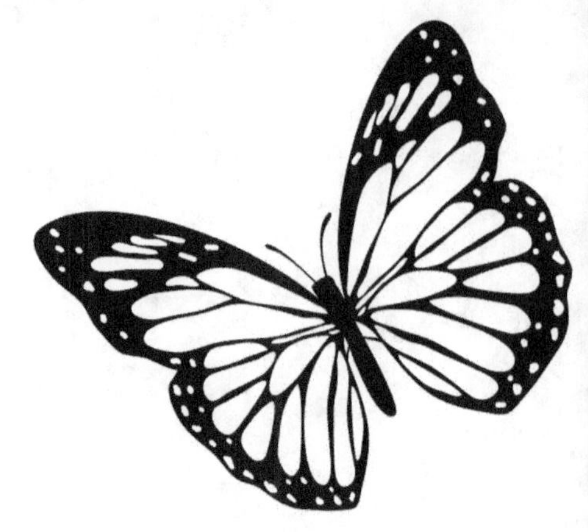

This Book Belongs to:

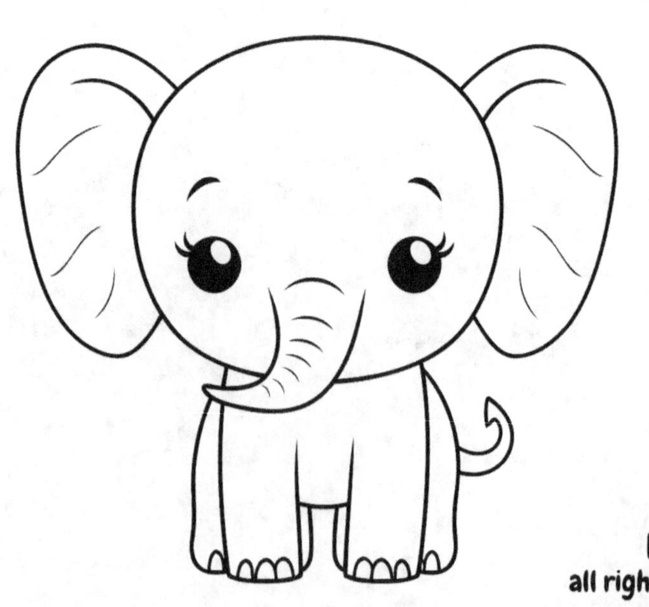
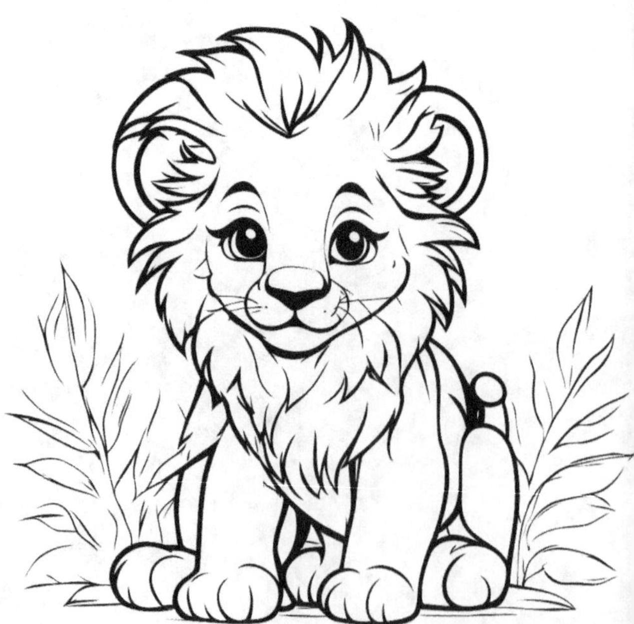

Test Color Page

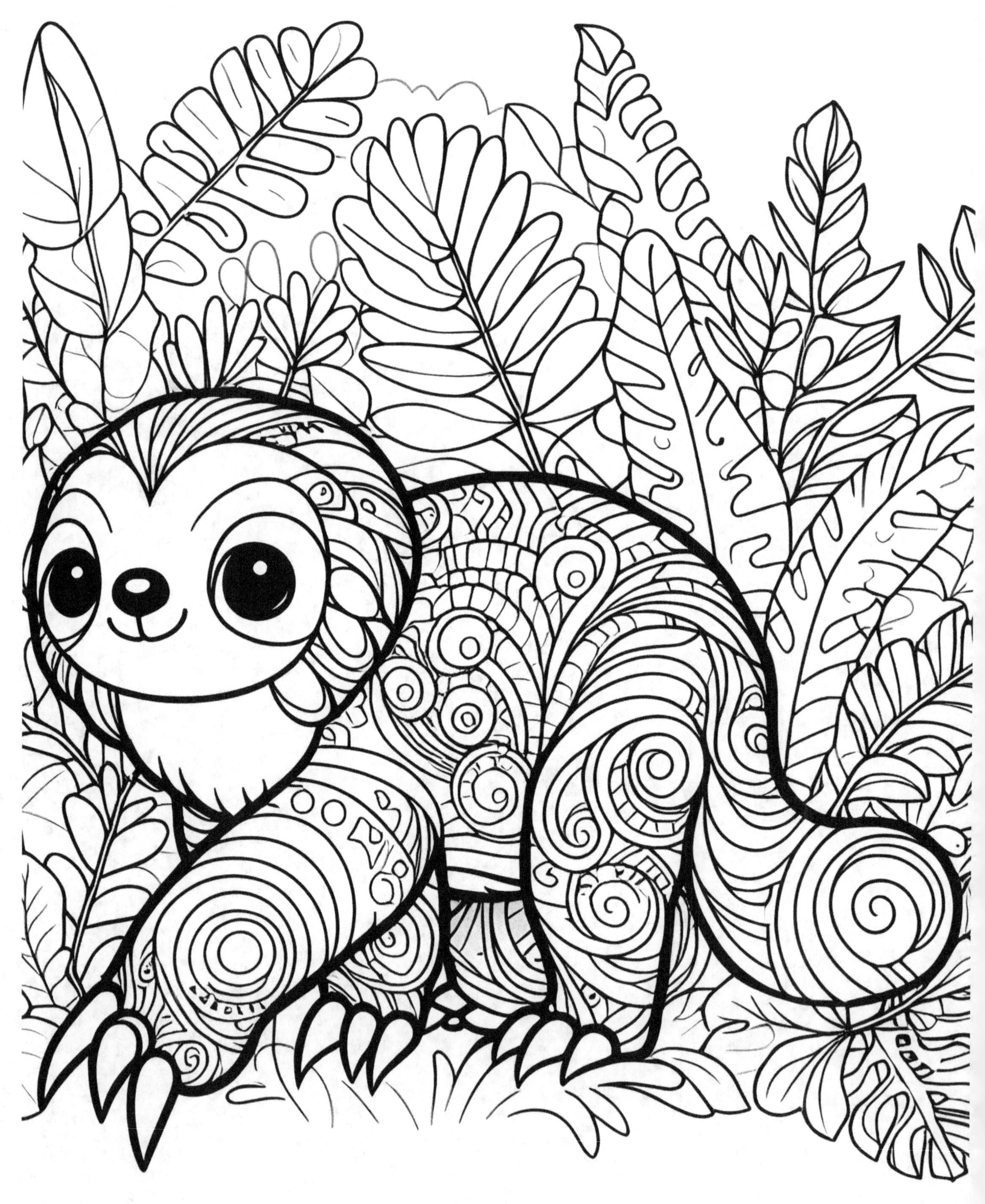

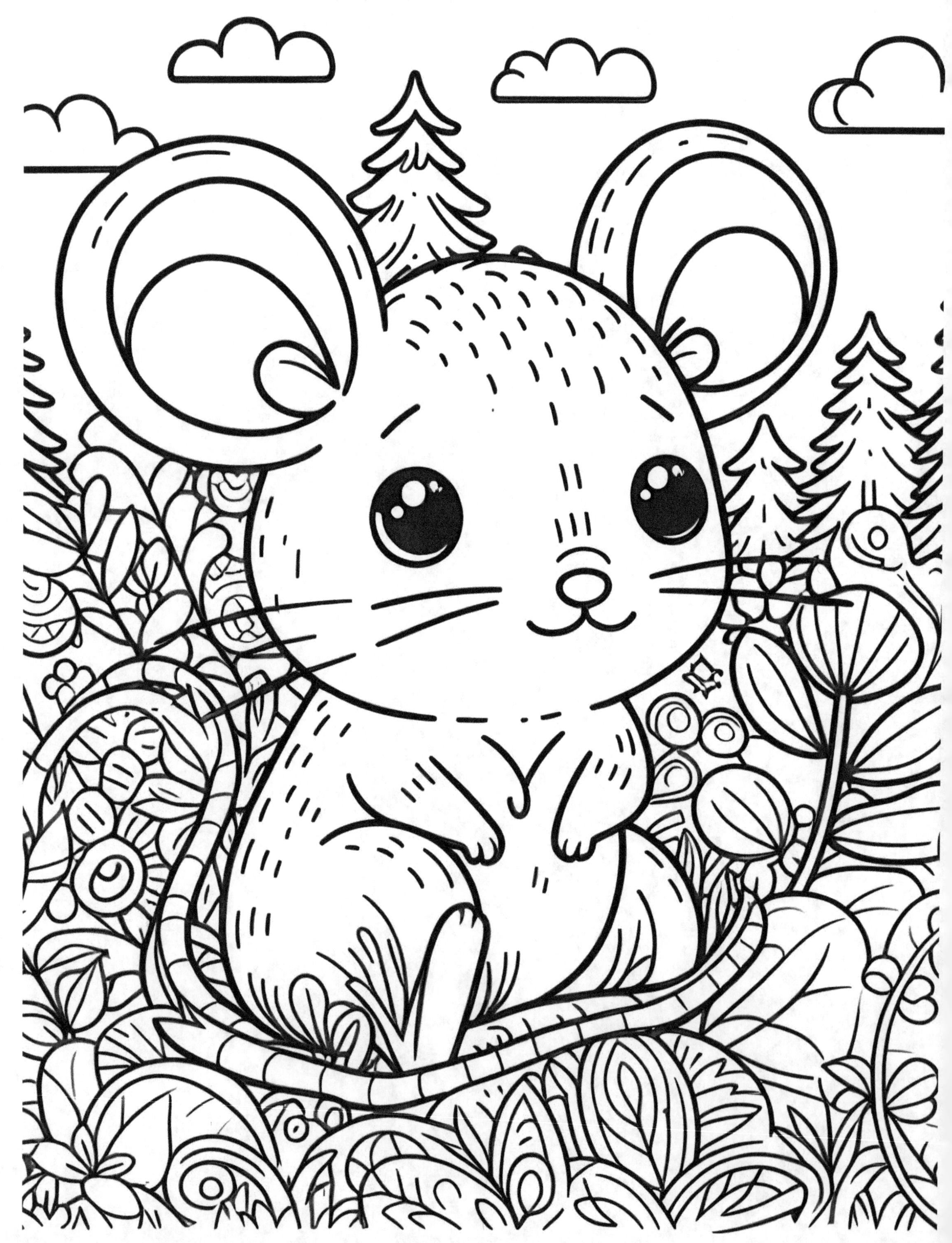

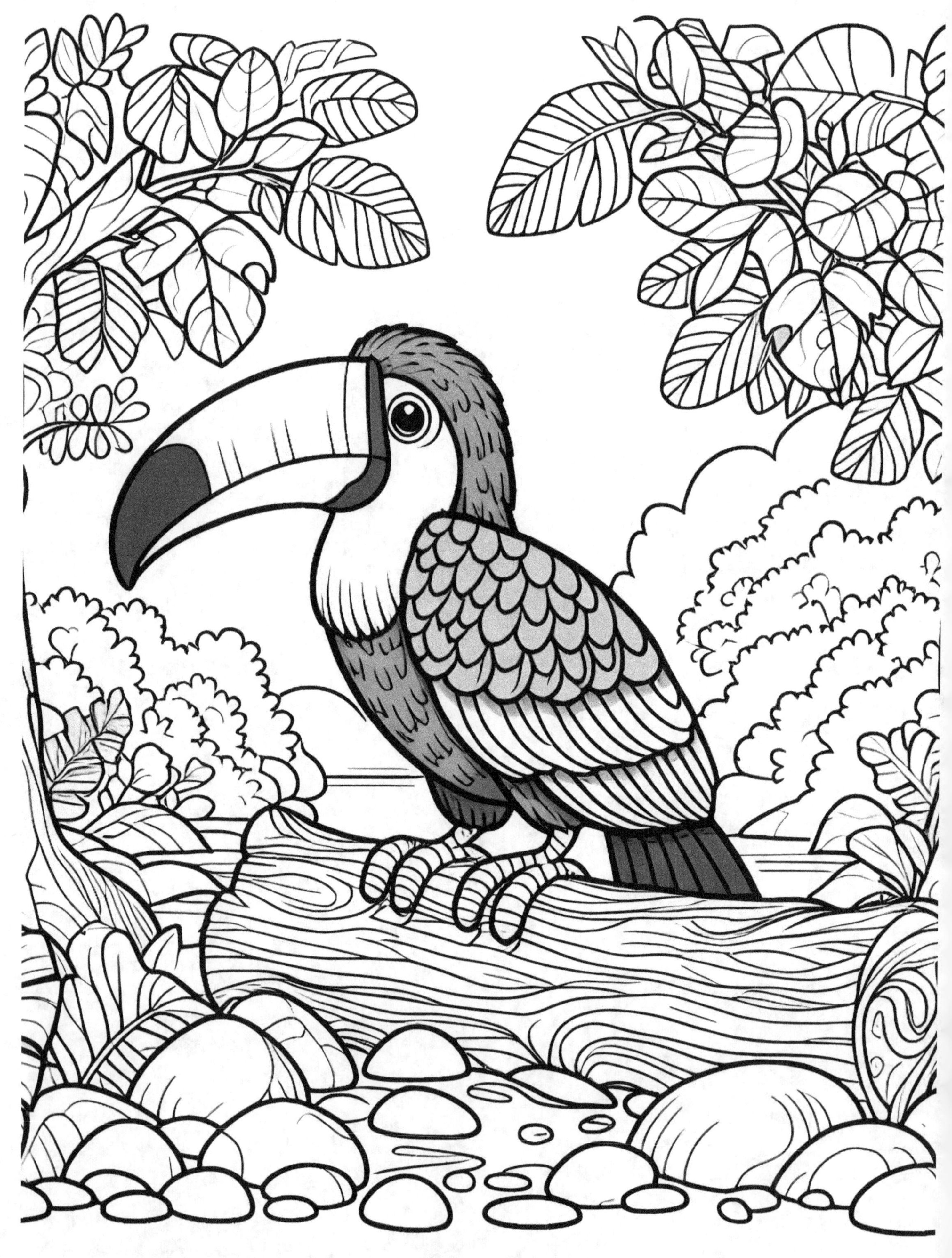

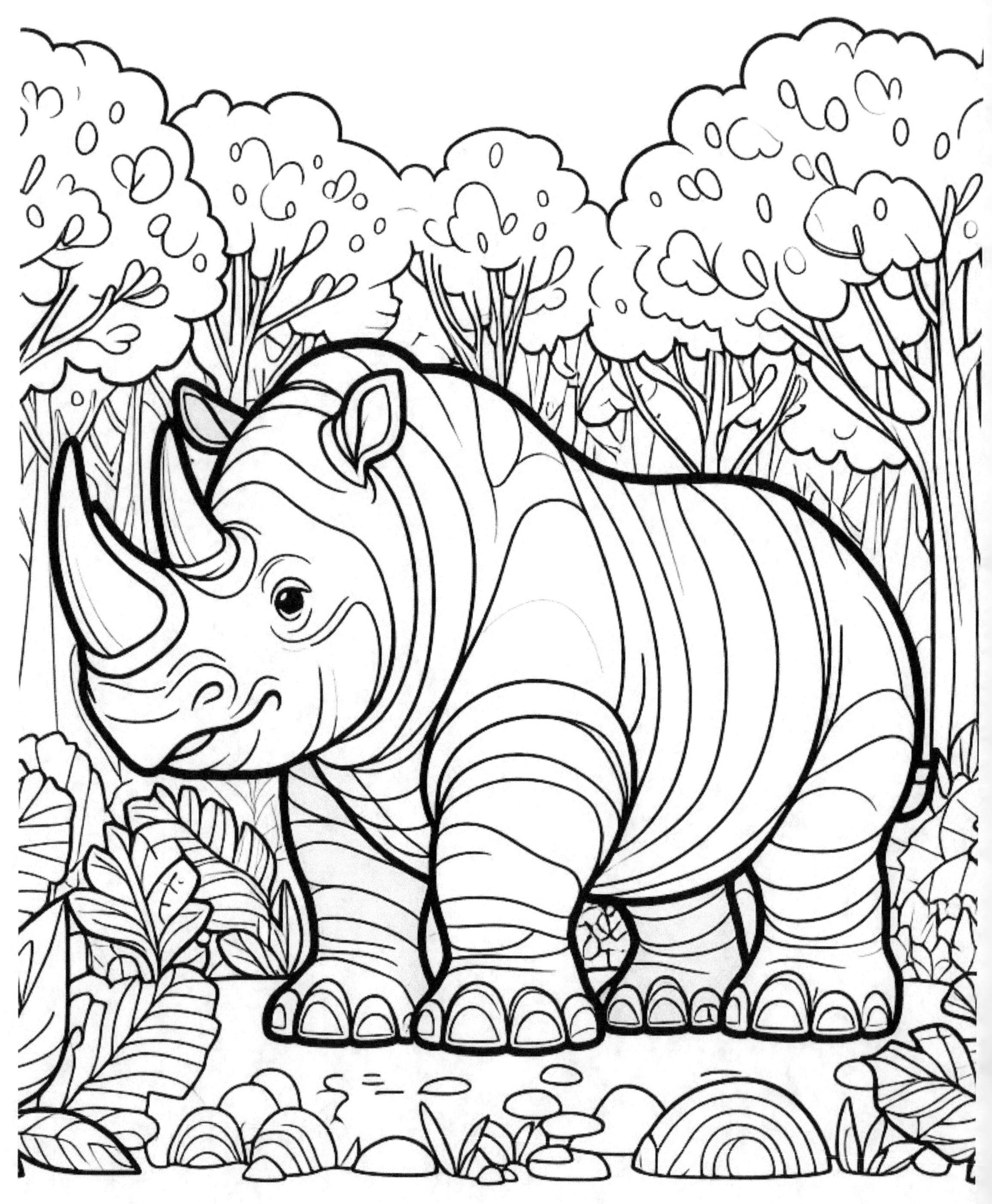

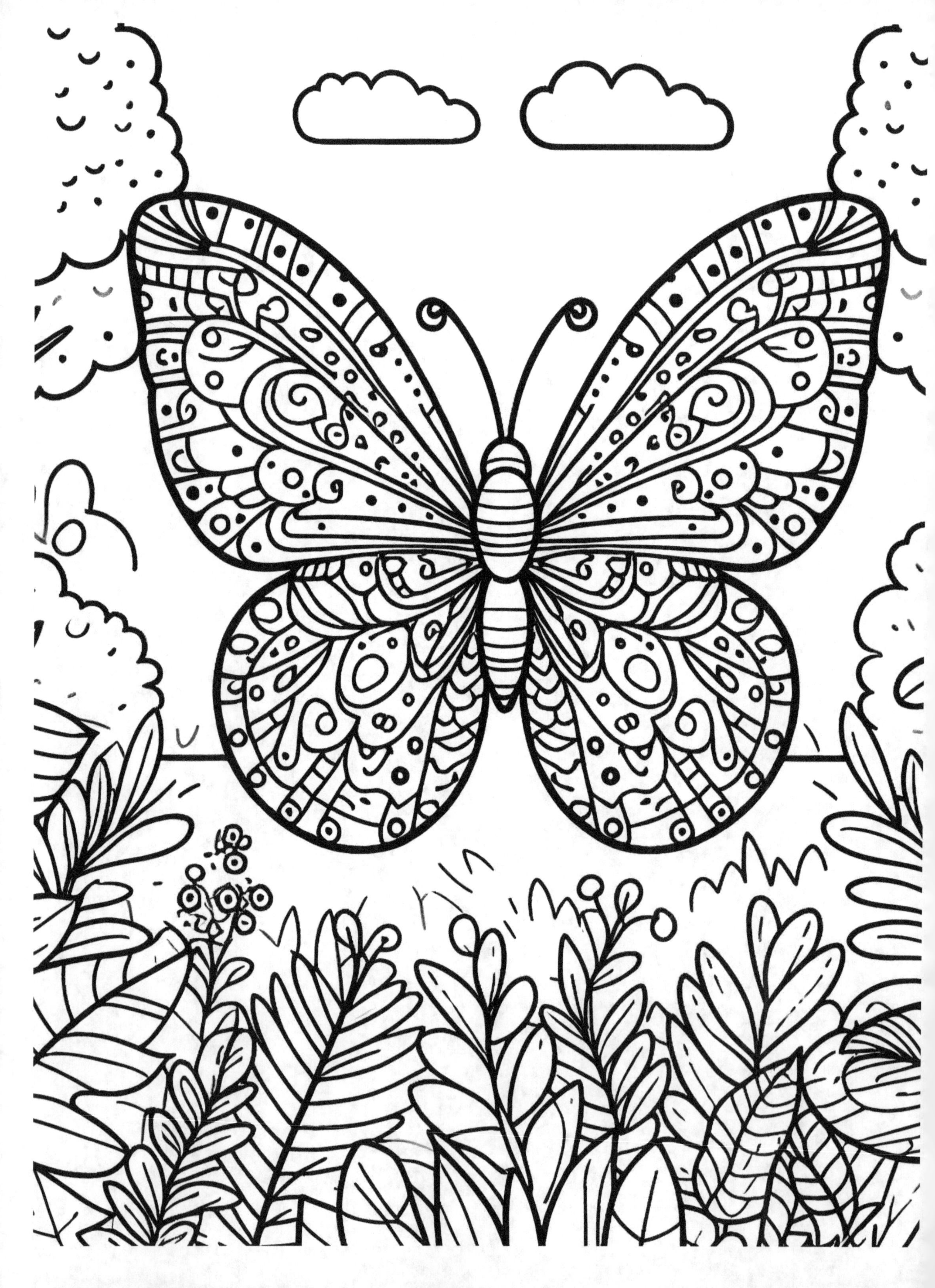

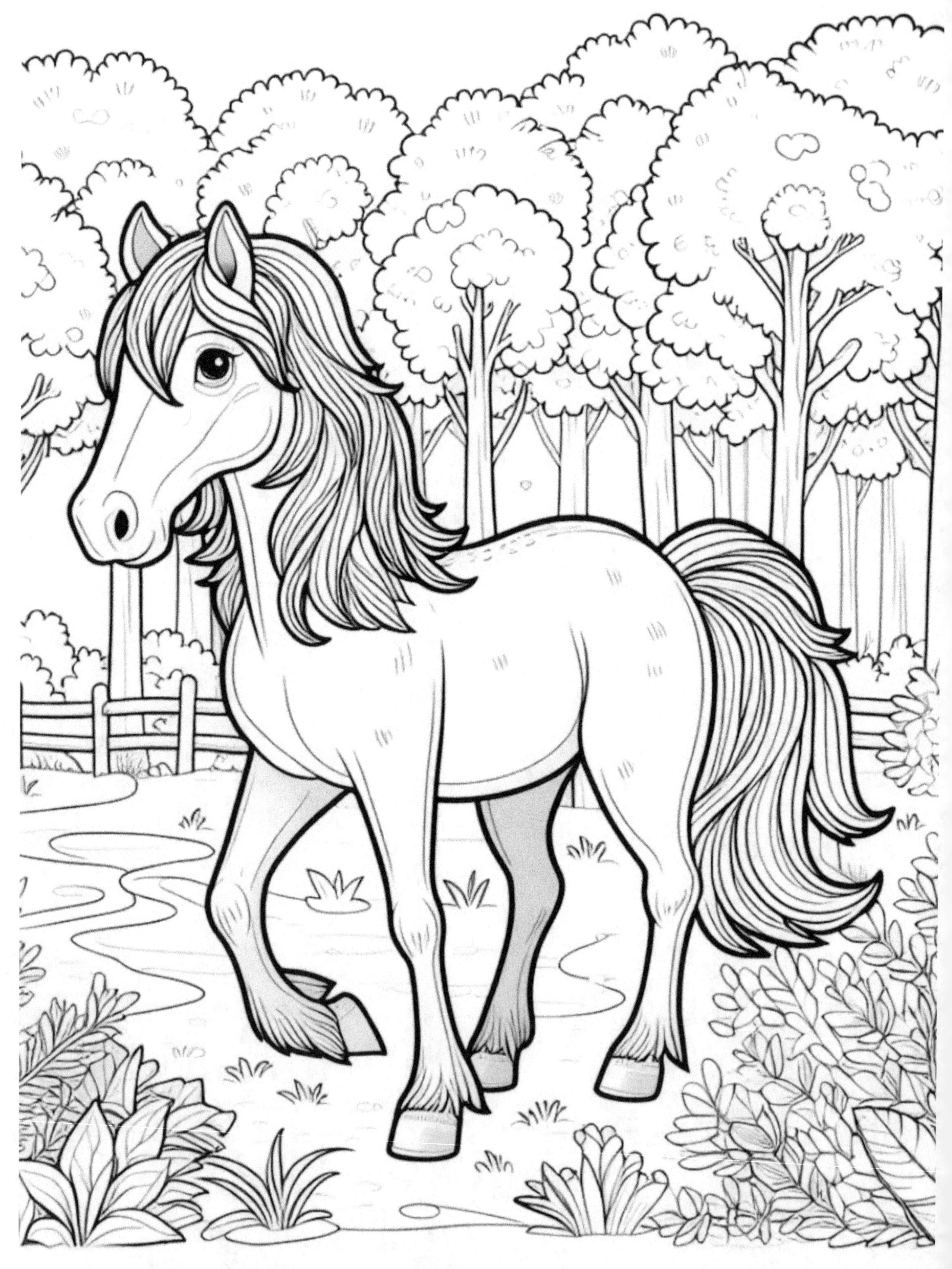

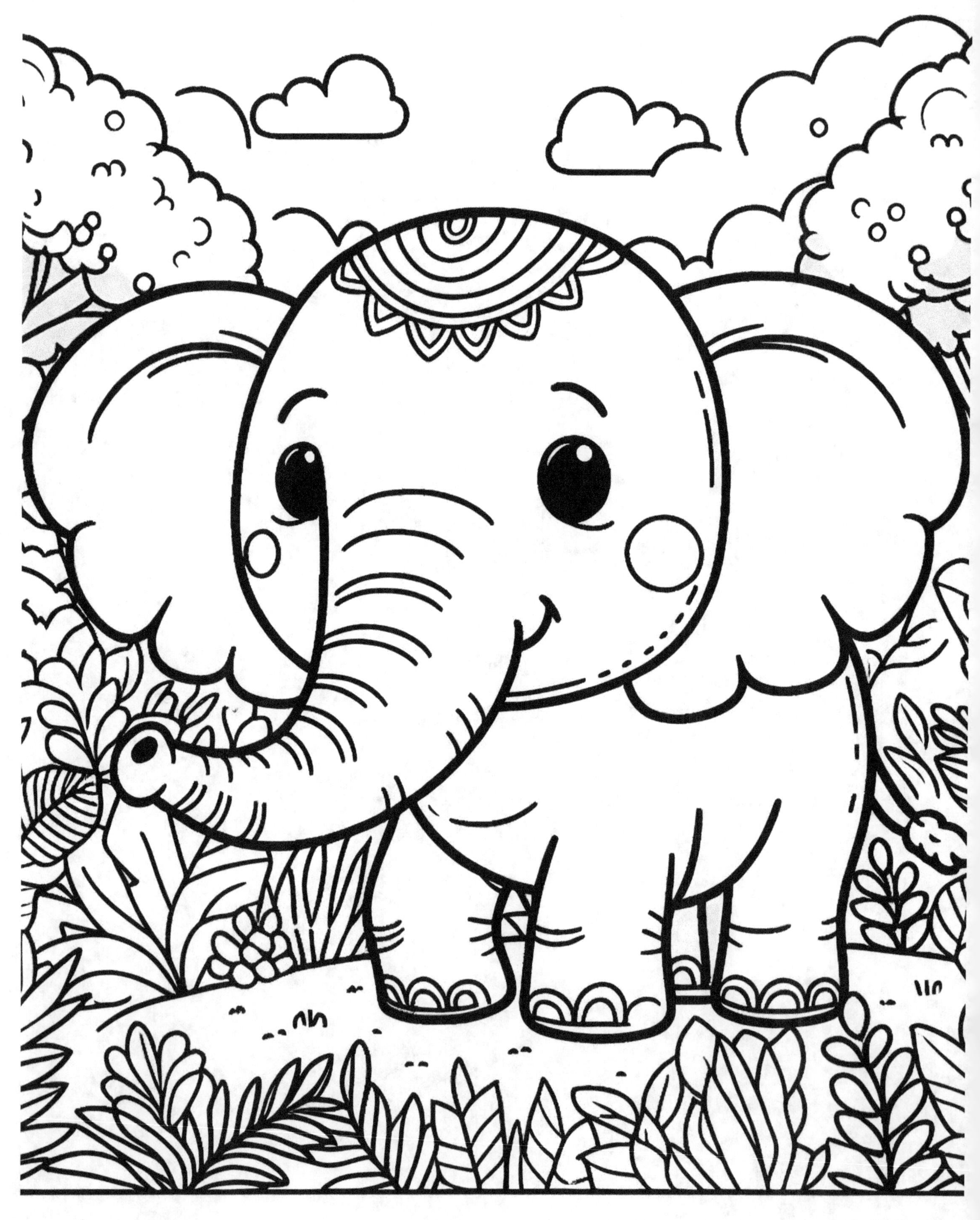

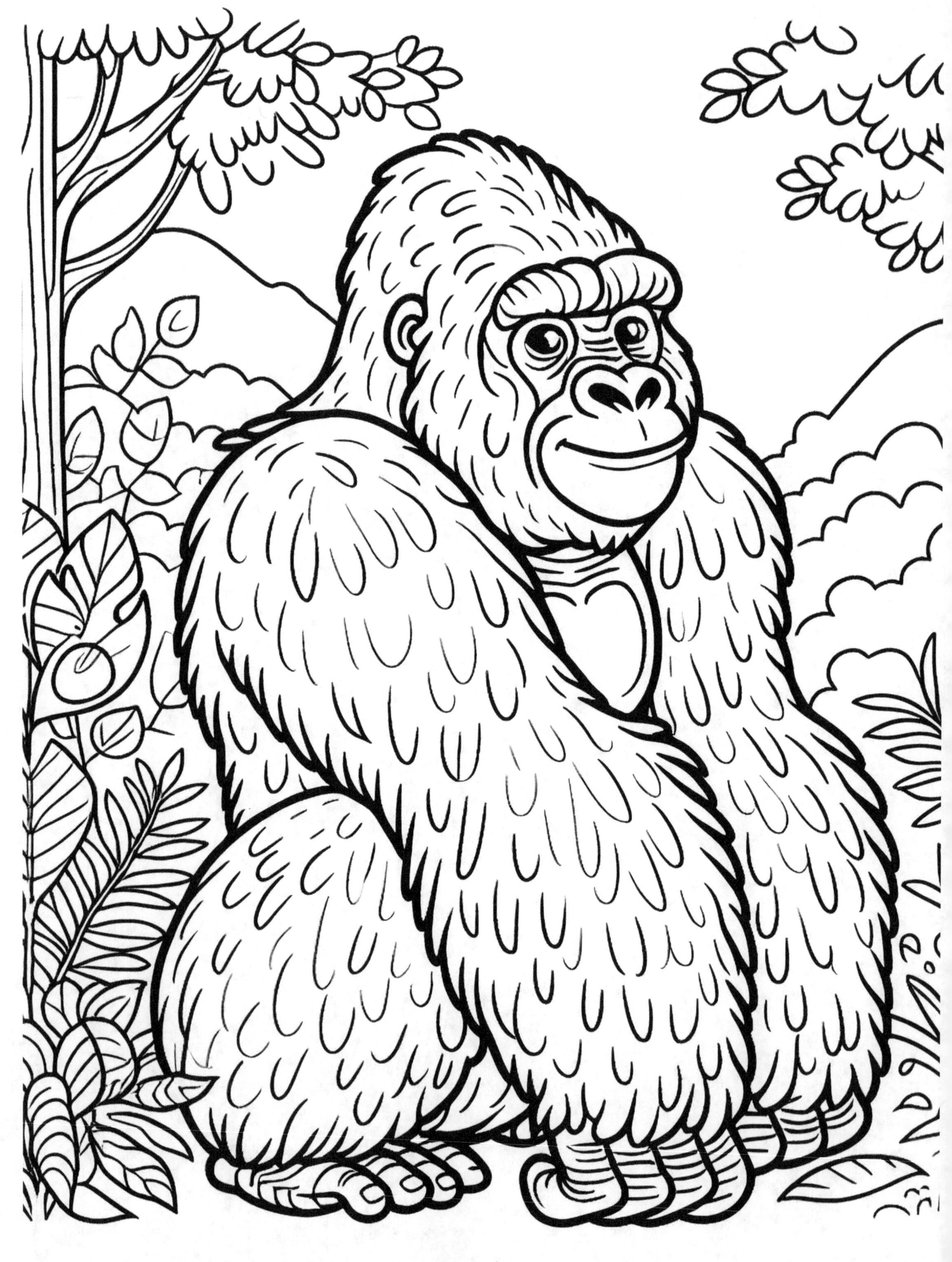

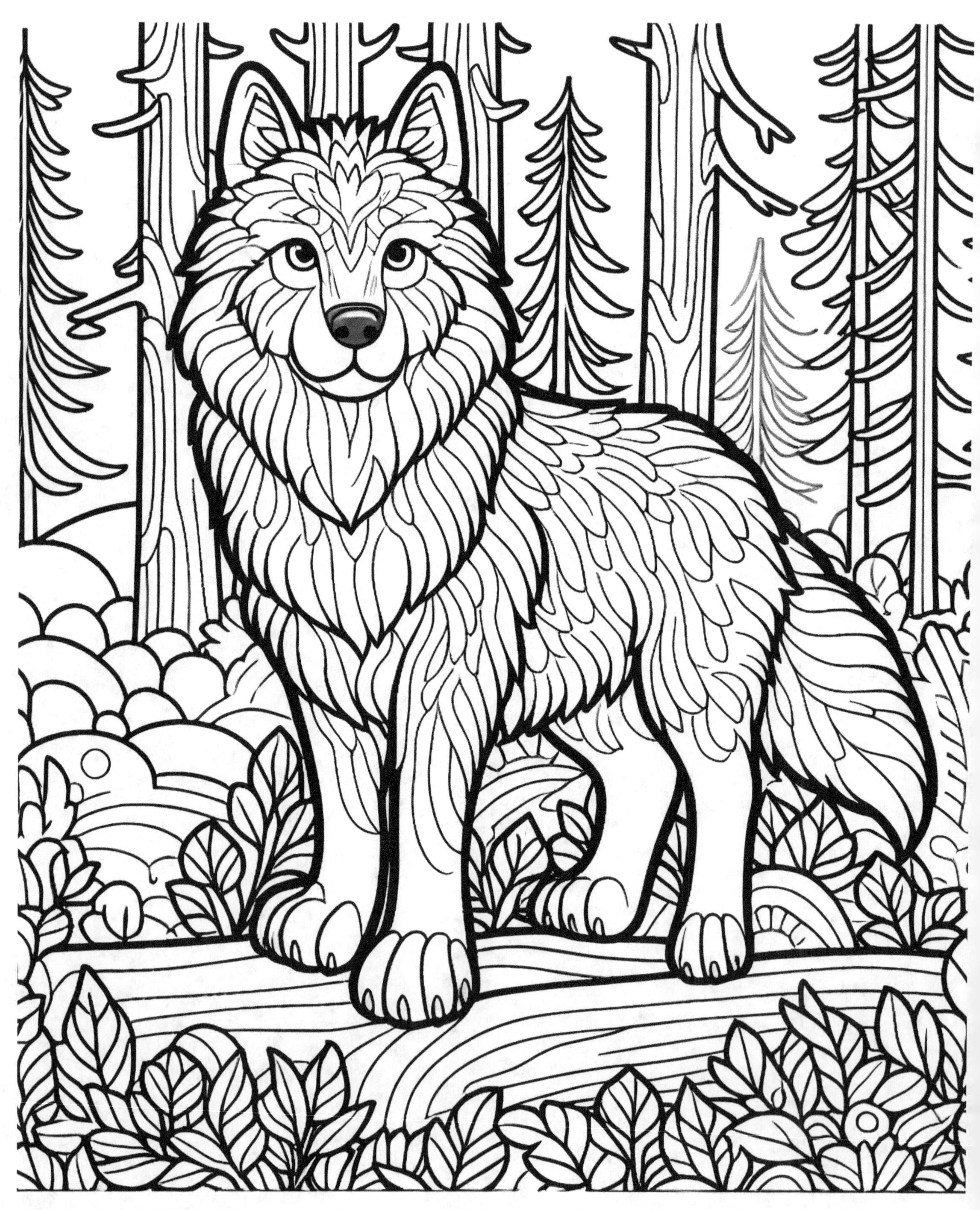

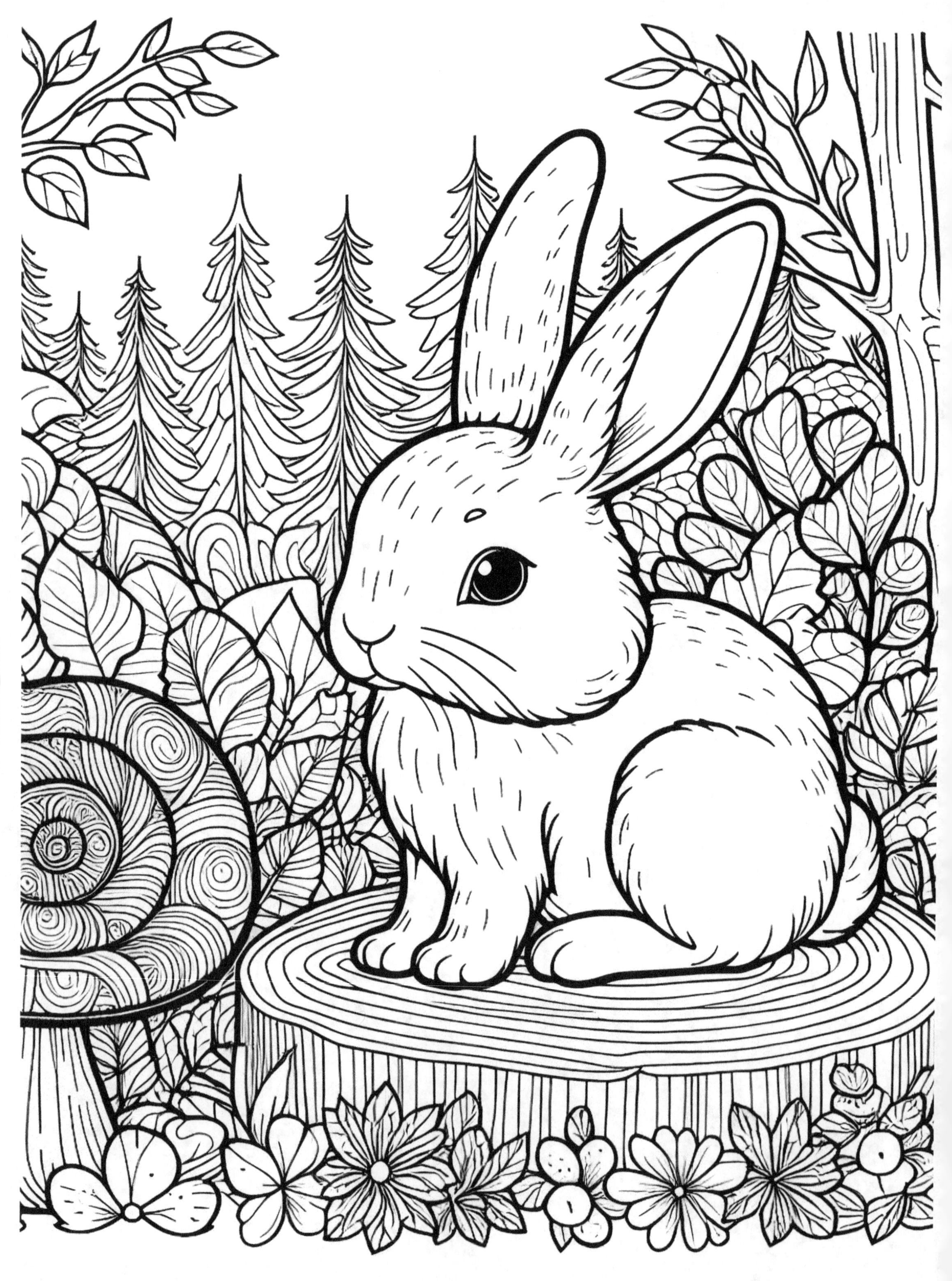

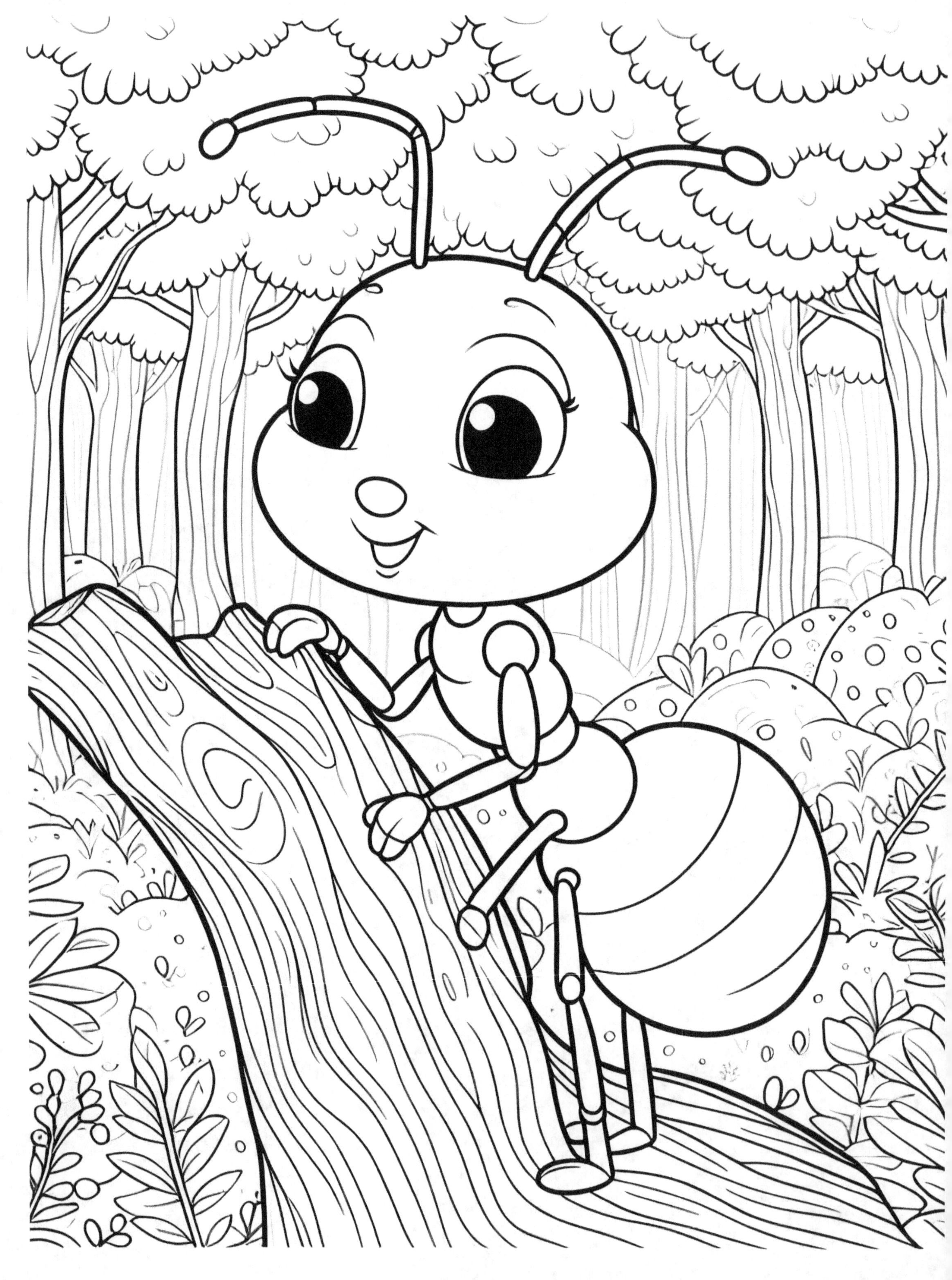

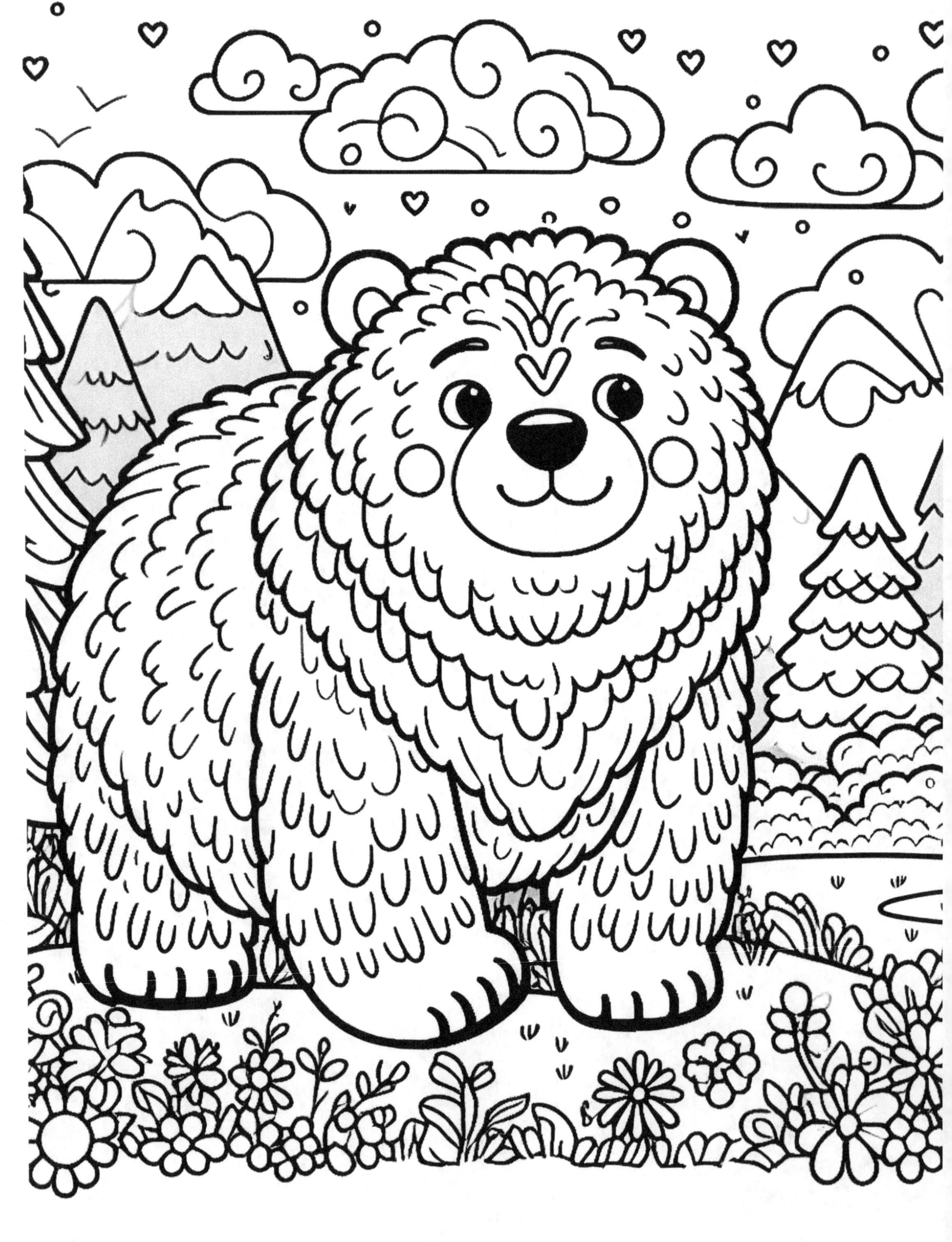

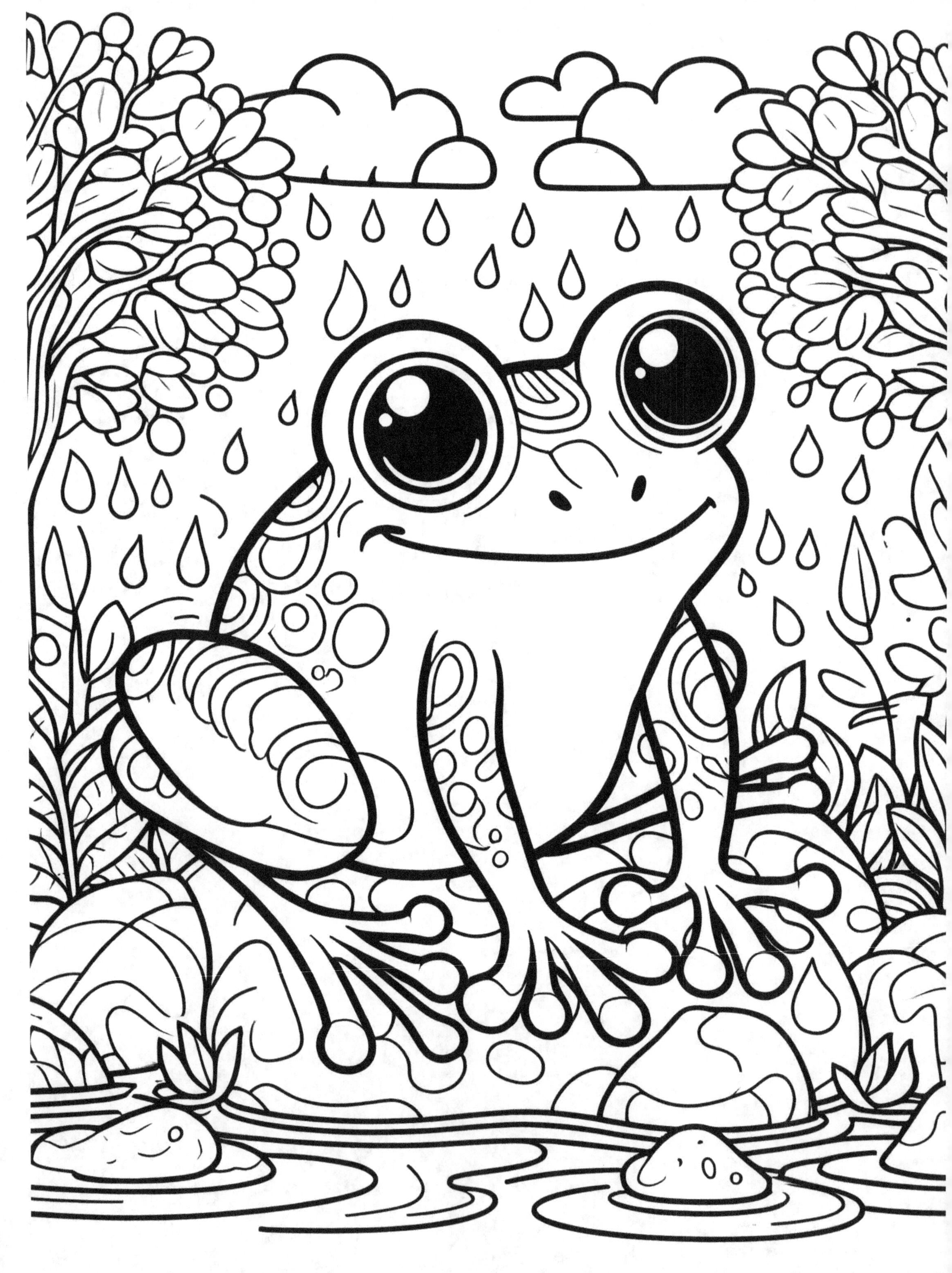

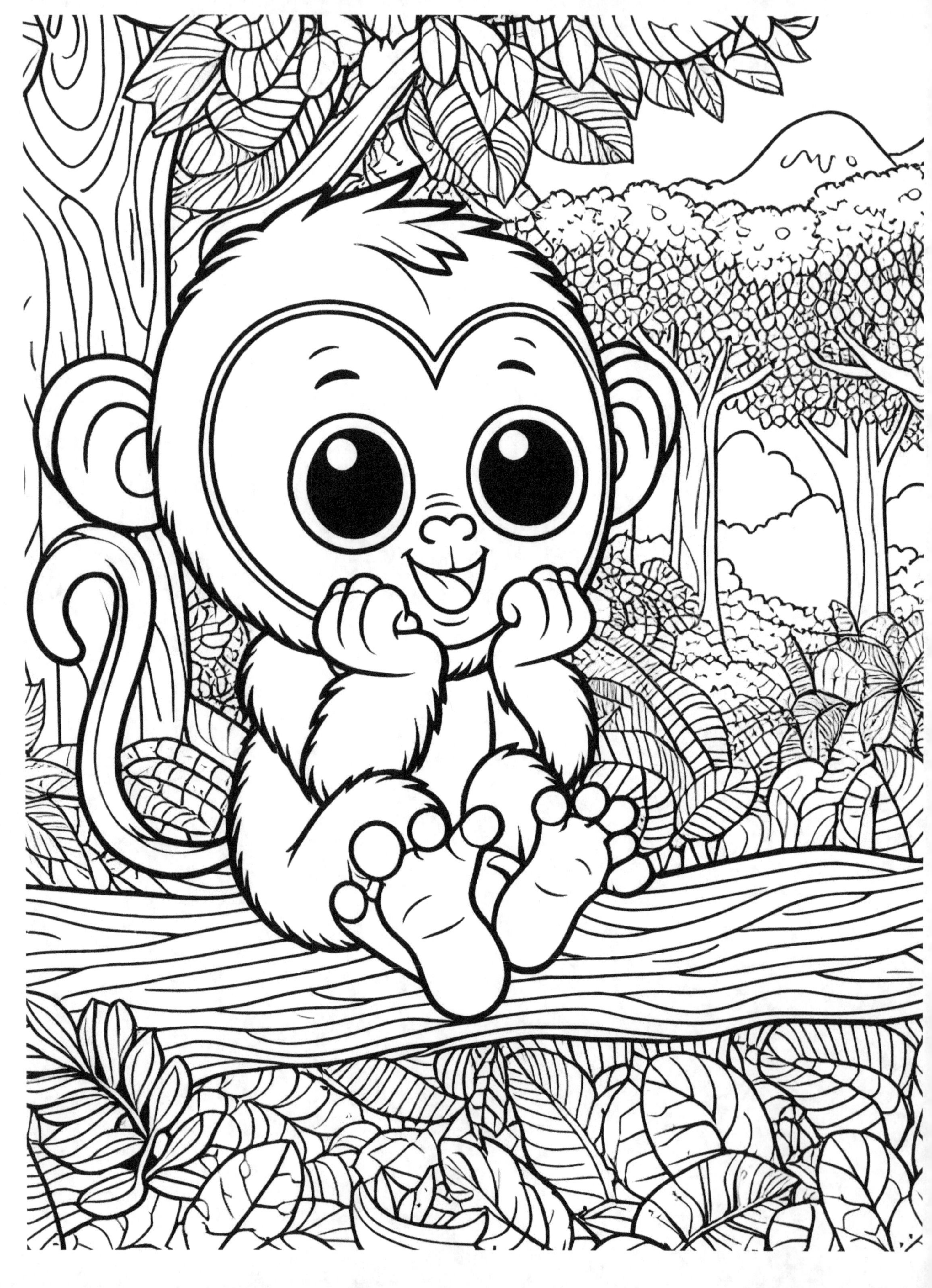

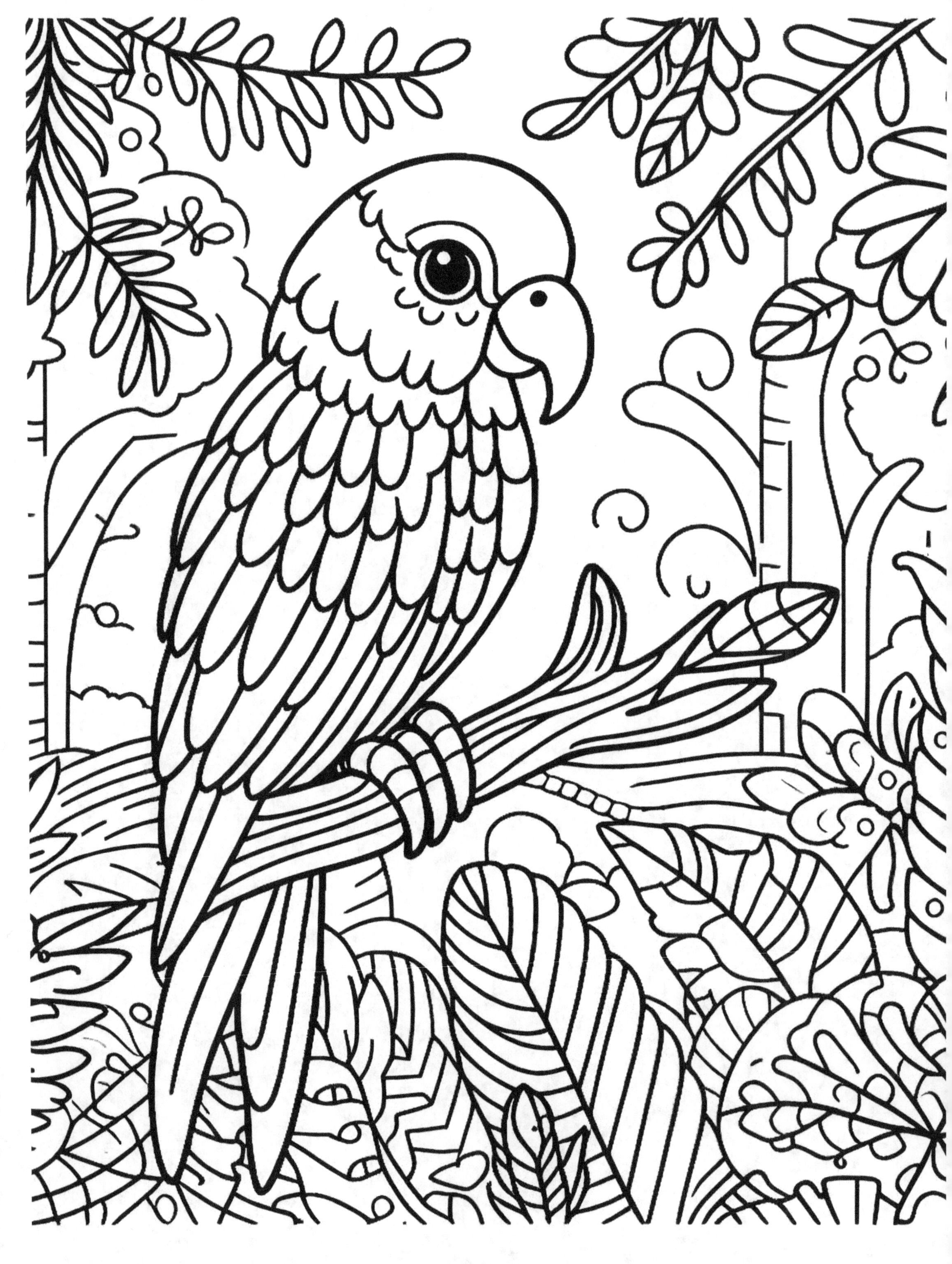

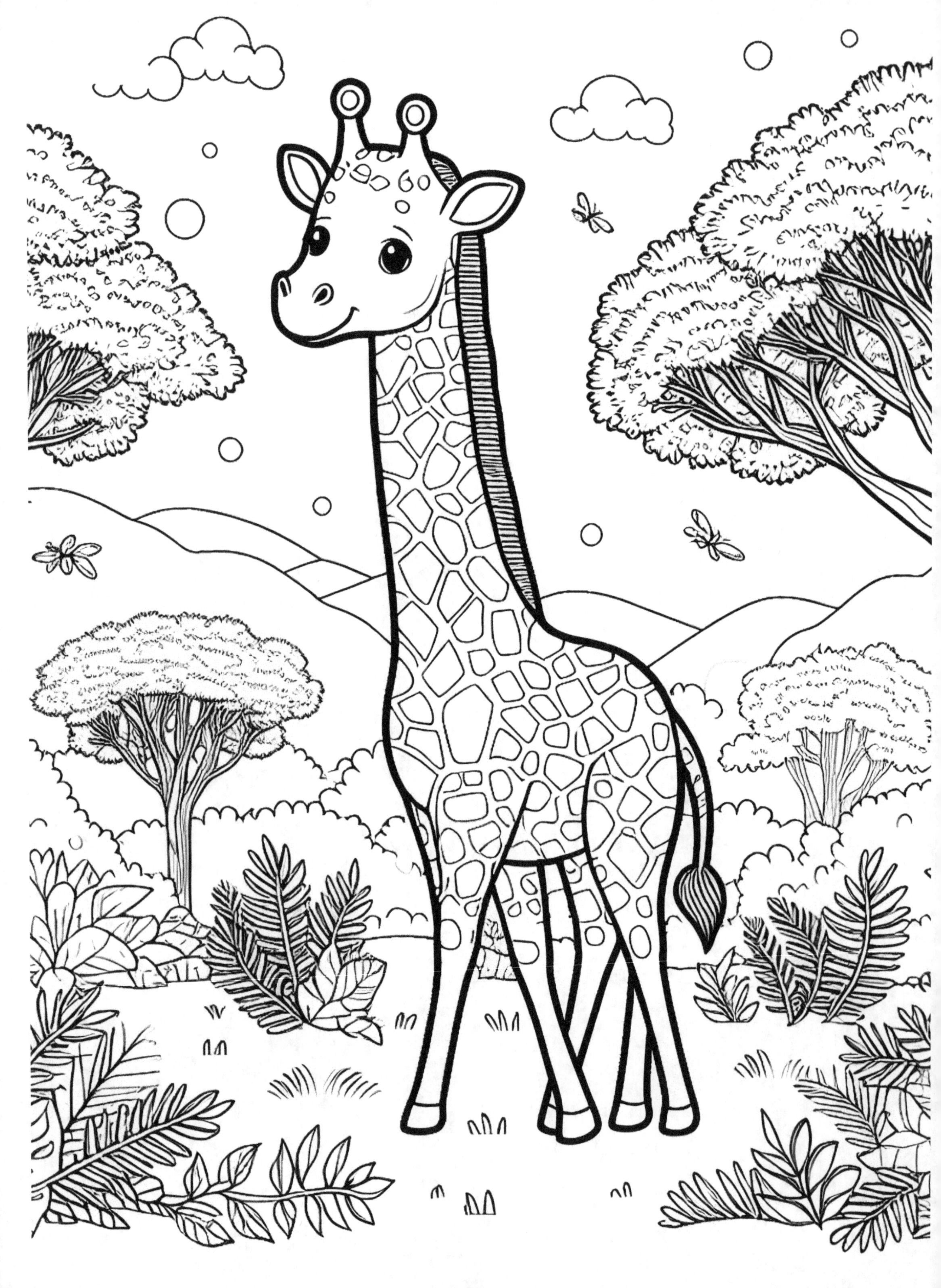

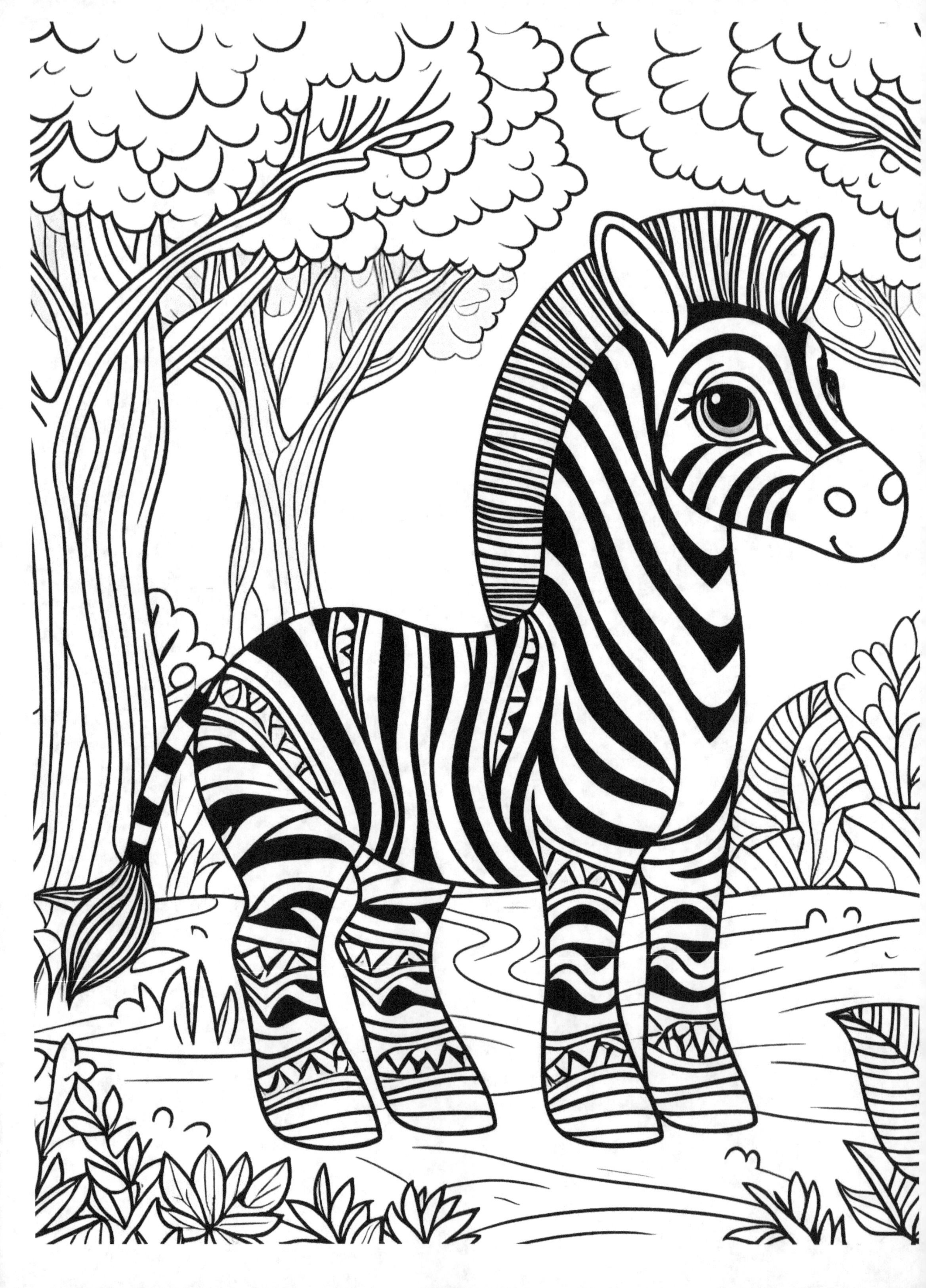

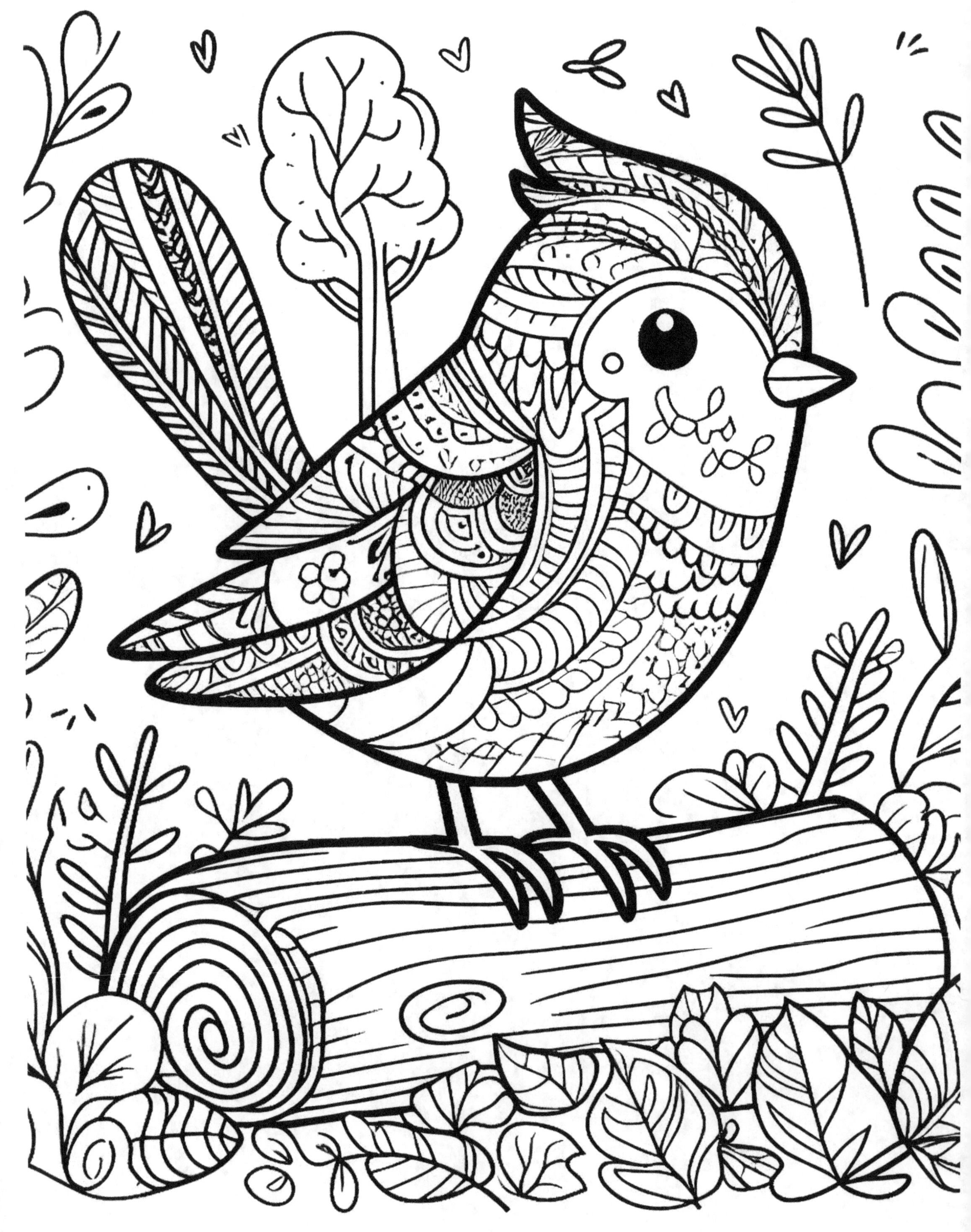

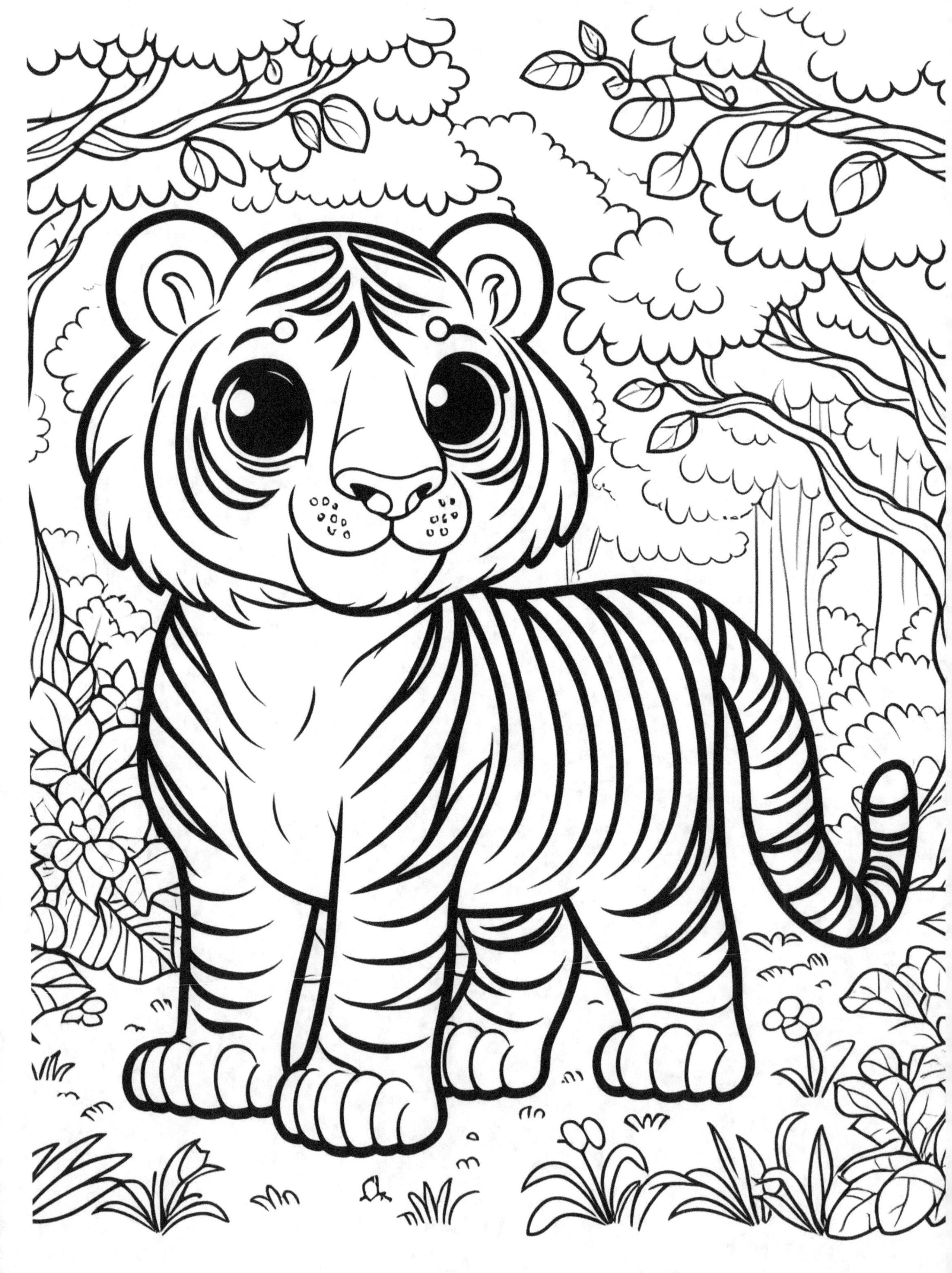

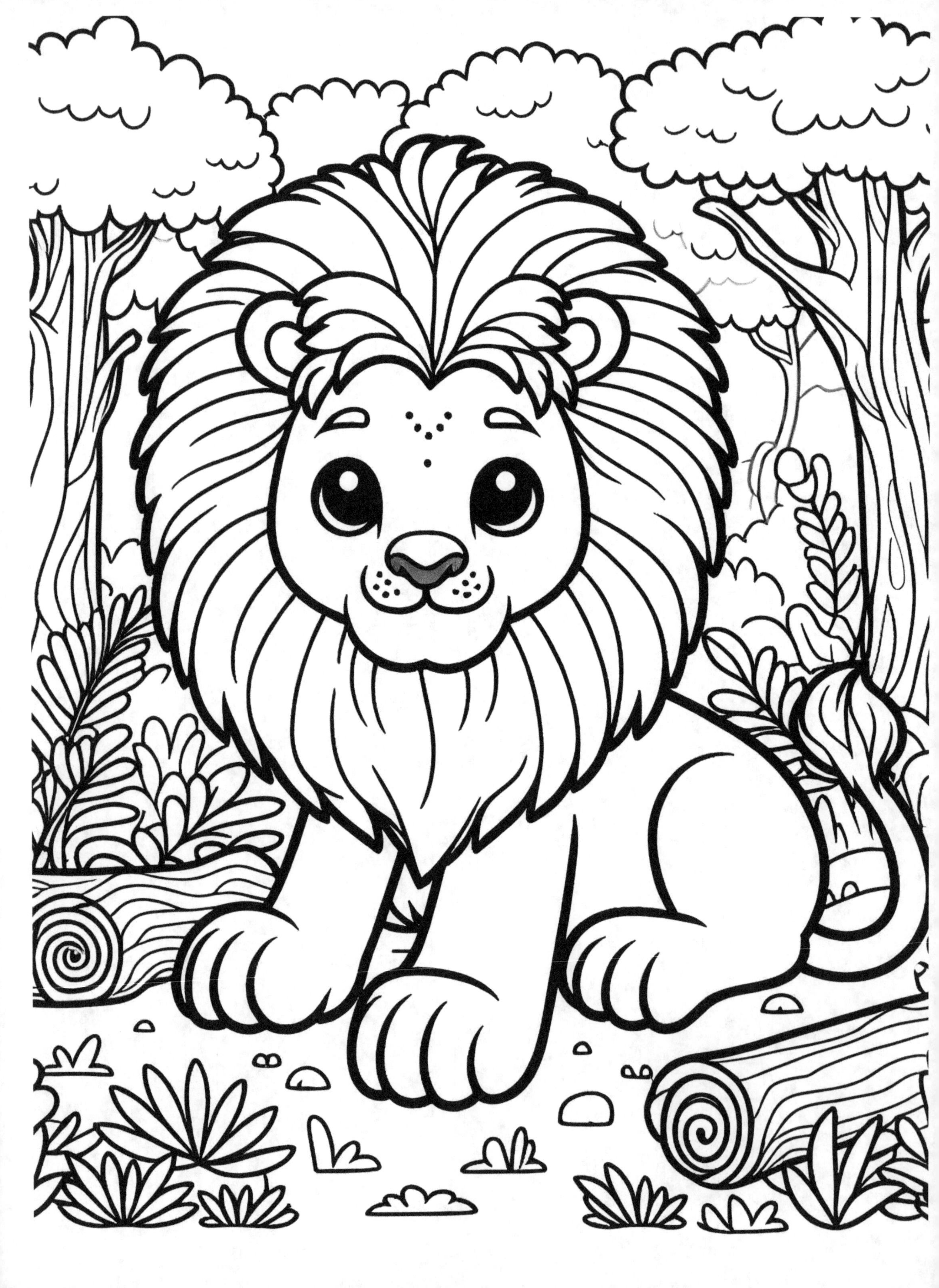